MG Z
CARS

Craig Cheetham

AMBERLEY

First published 2020

Amberley Publishing
The Hill, Stroud
Gloucestershire, GL5 4EP

www.amberley-books.com

Copyright © Craig Cheetham, 2020

The right of Craig Cheetham to be identified as the
Author of this work has been asserted in
accordance with the Copyrights, Designs and
Patents Act 1988.

ISBN 978 1 3981 0095 4 (print)
ISBN 978 1 3981 0096 1 (ebook)

British Library Cataloguing in Publication Data.
A catalogue record for this book is available from
the British Library.

Typeset in 10pt on 13pt Celeste.
Typesetting by SJmagic DESIGN SERVICES, India.
Printed in the UK.

Introduction

Desperate times call for desperate measures and, as desperate measures go, the MG 'Z Car' range was a pretty ambitious one.

The MG ZR, ZS and ZT were three sports saloons that between them kept a struggling car manufacturer on life support for almost five years, selling not only on the back of patriotic fervour from British buyers (which was rapidly diminishing), but also on merit for being fun to drive, great value and bursting with character. Yes, they were old-fashioned, but they were also quite cool – for a short while at least.

At a time when MG Rover's fight for survival was reliant on attracting external investment, the impetus fell on the company's engineers, designers and sales and marketing teams to show the world what they could do, and to do it with minimal investment. And that's what the Z Cars achieved.

Back when the ZR, ZS and ZT first appeared and the final chapter in the MG Rover story began, I was a motoring journalist on one of the UK's best-known car magazines, *Auto Express*. And as someone who has spent his entire life as a student of the British car industry, to be at the business end of the developments at Longbridge and watch the endgame evolve was fascinating and – ultimately – a little heartbreaking. Not least because, during the process, I met so many people who put their hearts and souls into trying to make MG Rover work, and who lived and breathed that fight.

I also drove these cars when new, attending MG Rover launch events and driving them alongside their contemporaries. I wasn't blinkered enough to believe they were the best cars in their class, but they did get under my skin – for unlike many of their rivals the MGs had character, as indeed did the people who built them and those who ran the company.

Today, these cars are up-and-coming classics. Entertaining, affordable drivers' cars that have personality in even more abundance than they have flaws (of which there are quite a few). I know this not least because I've owned many and – at the time of writing – have three ZSs and three ZTs.

I really hope you enjoy this book as much as I enjoyed writing it, and as much as I've enjoyed owning, driving and restoring my own MG Z cars to preserve just a small chapter of the story for future generations.

I also need to thank John Hemming, Peter Stevens and Kevin Jones for their contributions to this story; each played a pivotal but very different role and I'm grateful to them for each taking time to tell their part of the saga.

It would also be remiss of me to not also thank Keith Adams and the fabulous web resource www.aronline.co.uk, which is an essential source of facts, history and fascinating anecdotes from the archives of the British car industry. There's no other resource quite like it for motoring historians and I'm extremely grateful to Keith for allowing me to reference the site herein.

Craig Cheetham
Cambridgeshire
December 2019

The author's Trophy Blue ZS.

Rover and BMW – The Divorce

The pairing of Rover and BMW was always a difficult one. The German company took the reins at Longbridge in 1994, much to the surprise of many in the industry.

Rover Group had been put up for sale by British Aerospace in 1993 after the parent company decided it could no longer sustain the car firm while managing significant losses through its aerospace business – a situation not helped by defence cuts in British government.

The expected outcome was that Honda, which had formed a successful alliance with Rover Group over the past twelve years, would increase its stake in the business to become a 50 per cent shareholder, but while the Japanese company was still doing its due diligence, an unexpected bid from BMW came in.

The Munich company's chief executive, Bernd Pischetsrieder, was a well-documented Anglophile – indeed, he was the nephew of Mini designer Alec Issigonis – and he saw in Rover Group a great opportunity to broaden BMW's appeal. The family-owned business was performing strongly and had a reputation for making great, high-quality cars, but it was also a car manufacturer with a very linear model range. Three saloons, all similar in profile but different in size, plus a couple of oddball sports models weren't the ideal recipe for growth, whereas acquiring Rover would not only buy BMW some world-class engineering expertise (especially in the realms of front-wheel-drive chassis dynamics), but also give it access to four-wheel-drive technology via Land Rover, plus a presence in the small car and supermini markets.

Bernd Pischetsrieder (right) at the acquisition of Rover by BMW.

What BMW wasn't prepared for, though, was Rover's rather haphazard management, which wasn't wholly apparent when it first took over. There were also some concerns around the brand's 'legacy' products, not least because the new Rover 400 was developed off Honda architecture and the Japanese firm was so embittered by the BMW takeover that it ramped up the cost of the automatic transmission, the 1.6-litre D16 engine and some of the dashboard mouldings required to build the car, making it almost impossible for Rover to make a profit on.

A similar story applied to the Rover 600, which was largely based on the Honda Accord and used mostly Honda engines and transmissions, at great expense to Rover.

A hasty product review began and the proposed replacement for the Rover Metro – the 'R3' – instead became the 200 to reduce reliance on the Honda-based 400. The 600 was actively under-marketed and the larger 800 re-engineered to use Rover-only powertrains, including a new 2.5-litre 'KV6' unit that would power the new 'R40' saloon in development under BMW. Heavy discounting on 800s to tempt fleet customers away from the 600 added further to the sense of the smaller car being unloved by Rover's management after the Honda fallout, though it did continue to sell in limited numbers until 1999.

Meanwhile, the Metro was facelifted to disguise the fact that the new 200 was actually a large supermini rather than a small compact hatch. The 200 and 400 would, in revised form, become an integral part of the MG Rover story, but early on in their gestation they were marketed as premium cars as Rover tried to boost its image and balance its books in the face of intense scrutiny from German management.

By 1997, though, there were serious concerns starting to surface around the company's finances. BMW's shareholders, including the founding Quandt family that still owned the majority of the business, demanded a turnaround that never came, despite the launch of the new Rover 75 in 1998 – a car that was co-developed with BMW and even used one of the German company's engines in the form of the 2.0-litre diesel unit.

One of the main issues with Rover's financial performance was related to foreign exchange mechanisms – the UK's refusal to join the Euro having an impact on the value of sterling and making it increasingly expensive for BMW to invest in the brand.

At the Rover 75's reveal in 1998, Pischetsrieder took the unprecedented step of firing a shot across the bows at the British government, stating that without government support Rover would not survive. It would be the start of two years of wrangling that would see the business slowly get broken up as BMW tried to relieve itself of its 'English Patient'.

First to go was Land Rover, which in April 2000 was sold to Ford for £1.8 billion – £1 billion more than BMW had paid for Rover Group in the first place. BMW now had an SUV of its own in the X5, so determined the brand was no longer needed. In order to prepare the rest of the business for sale, it decided which bits to keep for itself – namely the MINI brand, the already heavily developed 'R50', which was the internal codename for the Mini replacement, the Cowley plant, and the Hams Hall engine factory it had paid for earlier on in its tenure of the company. The rest was unceremoniously put up for sale, with 2000 being a year of torrid uncertainty for Rover and its workers. There were new cars in the pipeline, but these were BMW's intellectual property and would only see the light of day if the right buyer was found.

It looked for a long time that such an outcome would not be forthcoming. The most likely buyer to come to the table in March 2000 was Alchemy Partners, a venture capital business led by Jon Moulton and Eric Walters, who had no previous car industry experience. From the outset, its vision was to end Rover's days as a volume manufacturer and concentrate instead on specialist sports models – a move that would lead to a massive contraction of its operations, a sell-off of many of its facilities and wholesale job losses. But there seemed little alternative.

By 15 March, a position of intent had been reached by both BMW and Alchemy and the proposed deal was made public the following day, subject to due diligence – to the surprise of the media and the British government.

Alchemy's plan was to revive MG and rename Rover 'The MG Car Company', recalling past glories and winding down the Rover brand at the end of its current model cycles. It thought the only way to make money was through huge cost reductions and focusing on low-volume, high-profit margin cars. Rover's days as a mainstream manufacturer would be numbered.

Naturally this would also bring about a massive wave of redundancies both within Rover and also its supplier network, which sent morale through the floor. It was a surprise, too, to the British government – indeed, the Trade and Industry Secretary, Stephen Byers, would end up playing a significant role in the coming months and years.

One of the lesser-known but most significant players in the birth of what became MG Rover was John Hemming, a Liberal Democrat councillor in the Yardley district of Birmingham, who rallied local businesses and government to try and raise a counter-bid. Central to this was former Rover MD John Towers, who worked for the Department of Trade and Industry (DTI) and was a member of the UK's Training and Enterprise Council.

Towers had previously considered putting a bid together to buy Rover Group via a conglomerate of British business leaders and had dismissed the idea as too difficult, but with the Alchemy announcement came a new-found desire to block the bid. Former Rover dealer principal John Edwards joined the bid and within a week of the Alchemy/BMW announcement, Towers and some of his associates had sent a proposal called 'Project Phoenix' to Richard Burden, the MP for Longbridge.

What happened next was unprecedented in the history of the motor industry – and it all began with a fax...

Within days of BMW announcing its intentions to partner with Alchemy and rid itself of its 'English Patient', a far more diverse plot was being put together with the charismatic John Hemming playing the media and politicians off against each other to lead them to the belief that Rover could be saved.

Indeed, while it was the Phoenix Consortium and its self-appointed leader, John Towers, that later received a hero's welcome in south-west Birmingham, it was Hemming who was the man who probably saved Rover – at least in the first instance. Arguably, his influence on the next five years of British car manufacturing was immense, making him one of the industry's most unlikely and unsung heroes.

After attending a debate on Central Television, during which opposing MPs Julie Kirkbride (Conservative) and Richard Burden (Labour) blamed each other for the state of Rover Group, Hemming took to the local media to call for collaboration rather than contradiction – a rallying call that won the backing of the unions.

With their support, Hemming contacted union boss Tony Woodley and was advised that the way forward was to put in some form of written offer to BMW as soon as possible, so Hemming contacted the Germans via fax the very same day, explaining that a consortium bid was being put together and that a window of opportunity was needed in order to pull together the finer details.

At this stage, John Towers was keeping the project at arm's length – his involvement with the DTI meaning he didn't want to get involved just yet.

Meanwhile, the UK's Trade and Industry Secretary Stephen Byers met with BMW's top management in Munich to discuss a way forward, with Chris Woodwark – former head of Rolls-Royce Motor Cars – named as the future head of the MG Car Company under Alchemy.

John Towers.

BMW chairman Joachim Milberg with DTI's Stephen Byers (left).

While this was ongoing, Hemming and his team hit a roadblock in that BMW wouldn't share any financial information around Rover Group due to a memorandum of confidentiality it had signed with Alchemy Partners, and the only way around this was for any other interested party to formalise an offer to buy the company.

Negotiations in the UK continued apace. John Towers – in his DTI role – arranged a meeting with Nick Stephenson, whom he had worked with previously at Perkins Engines. A former manufacturing boss, it was Stephenson to whom Towers looked to see if there was a viable future for volume manufacturing at the Longbridge factory. It wasn't Stephenson's first discussion with BMW around the future of Rover, either – as a non-executive director of Lola Motorsport he'd previously made an approach along with Mayflower (which produced MGF bodyshells at its factory in Coventry) to buy the MG brand, but had been knocked back.

On the morning of 27 March 2000, the future of Rover would take on a very new shape. With the backing of the DTI and the unions, John Hemming faxed an offer to BMW at 6.00 a.m. stating that a consortium takeover bid was nearly ready and that a business plan was pretty much good to go, although any offer to buy the company from BMW would be 'nominal' and subject to full visibility of Rover Group's accounts.

John Edwards, meanwhile, confirmed that he had also been trying to establish a consortium via the dealer network, but had not managed to raise sufficient interest. John Hemming decided that the only way forward was to bring together all sides who wanted to counter-bid Alchemy, using strength in numbers to convince BMW it was the way forward. A further boost to the bid came from union leader Tony Woodley, who confirmed that the trades unions had obtained an agreement from BMW that any funding or 'dowry' offered on completion of an external deal would match that offered by Alchemy.

On the final day of March 2000, a meeting took place that would prove critical for Rover Group's future. Attending were Hemming, John Towers, John Edwards, Peter Beale, Andrew Sparrow (a lawyer), and representatives from both unions and finance partners.

The conversation was fraught and Hemming, along with Carl Chinn, a professor of economics and local community champion, left the meeting early after several disagreements. By the time the meeting concluded, the new business plan – Project Phoenix – was born.

Initially, the Phoenix bid included the new MINI (who knows how things may have transpired if MG Rover had included the small car in its new portfolio?) but BMW insisted it had to keep the MINI, Triumph and Austin-Healey brands. Irrespective, Towers decided to resign from the DTI to officially head-up the Phoenix Consortium.

John Hemming made a momentary comeback, introducing Phoenix to potential backers through financial institutions he'd worked with while running his own company, but he would never again lead the bid.

Meanwhile, Alchemy was in advanced negotiations with BMW and by mid-April 2000 still looked like the most likely winner in the battle to take over the remains of Rover Group. Its business plan was simpler, its profitability more likely and its future potentially more secure – but they were getting cold feet. After six weeks of due diligence, Alchemy had uncovered contractual agreements with suppliers, dealers and employees to which it couldn't commit, so escalated talks with BMW to secure more financial backing to negotiate their way out of any awkward comeback.

On April 27 2000, Jon Moulton and Eric Walters met BMW's solicitors to discuss their concerns around the risk of legal or industrial action as a consequence of BMW's failure to give unions acceptable warning of its plans to dispose of Rover. Also, BMW would only guarantee statutory minimum redundancy payments to the 4,000 employees that Alchemy planned to lay-off, whereas Moulton knew that in order to avert serious industrial action, the offer would need to be higher.

Because of this, Alchemy believed it would need an extra £100 million or so on top of the original £500 million payment tabled to BMW in order to take Rover off its hands. In itself, this was not enough to scupper the Alchemy-BMW deal, but when BMW argued that Alchemy would have to guarantee £1 billion of loans to the Rover distribution network the discussions collapsed. The deal was off.

This led to scenes of euphoria within the Rover workforce. The Alchemy bid was never going to be good news for the 6,700 employees at Longbridge as it meant two-thirds of them would lose their jobs, and now BMW only had one clear option to dispose of Rover without the expense of closing it.

Just four days after the Alchemy deal collapsed, John Towers and Nick Stephenson met up with BMW's solicitors, and as with Alchemy, BMW offered Phoenix a £500 million dowry to take over the running of Rover and Longbridge – but BMW remained concerned at the lack of a financial backer for Phoenix, and asked Towers how he could build over 200,000 cars per year without financial support.

The Germans' concerns caused major problems for the bid. The DTI, which had originally been supportive of the plan, did a complete U-turn as soon as it became apparent that the government may have to pick up the tab for the company's collapse (possibly because Towers himself no longer worked for the DTI), so it backtracked on any government support, leaving Phoenix with a business plan and a board, but not enough money to see its plans through.

The funding to deliver the plan eventually came from the First Union Bank of North Carolina, which offered £200 million of working capital to get the new project underway. But why an American bank? Was it pure coincidence that BMW's new flagship SUV factory was at Spartanburg in neighbouring South Carolina?

MG Rover was finally founded in May 2000.

Irrespective, Phoenix was back in business – and on 8 May 2000, Towers and BMW's lawyers met to agree the deal. That night, Rover was handed over to Phoenix for the nominal sum of £10, and in return, the company would receive £500 million from BMW, which would cover the costs of redundancies and company restructuring.

John Towers made Nick Stephenson, John Edwards, and Peter Beale company directors – the infamous 'Phoenix Four', who would later go on to be the subject of one of the UK's most intensive corporate inquiries.

But for now, the newly formed MG Rover was looking to the future and the future alone.

On 9 May, Towers returned from Birmingham Airport in a chauffeur-driven Rover 75 to a hero's welcome at Longbridge's iconic 'Elephant House' headquarters, where he was mobbed by workers and media alike.

'It's a very satisfactory outcome for us and it's an emotional day,' he told the crowds. 'We have a huge amount of work to do to get the cash flow into a positive balance. We are determined to do that.'

The task ahead for 'Phoenix Venture Holdings Limited' (as it had become) looked difficult, but the feeling of optimism that Towers managed to generate was infectious. An entirely new management structure was brought in to form MG Rover Group Ltd, and with it came a renewed enthusiasm for the MG and Rover brands.

Never before had the company's design, engineering, manufacturing and marketing teams worked more eagerly, closely or enthusiastically to bring new models to market, which given their budget constraints was not an easy task.

Chief among them was something that BMW had wilfully obstructed through its tenure of Rover Group – that being a range of performance saloons based on the existing model range and wearing the iconic octagon of MG.

Enter the Z Cars...

John Hemming – An Unlikely Hero?

Without John Hemming, there's every chance that the writing could have been on the wall for MG Rover in 2000 and the Z cars would never have seen the light of day. It was Hemming who brought together all of the partners that made up the Phoenix bid, though on reflection he's not convinced it was all a good thing.

'In short, I think my biggest mistake was involving John Towers,' said Hemming as he recalled the time he brought the bid together. The former Liberal Democrat MP for Yardley was, at the time, deputy leader of Longbridge Council and also a successful local businessman.

On Friday 31 March 2000, with the clock ticking against Rover Group's future, he pulled together interested investors in that famous meeting. Himself, Towers, John Edwards, Peter Beale, lawyers, investors and union representatives. Among them were Mike Whitby, leader of Birmingham City Council, and Carl Chinn, Professor of Community History at Birmingham University.

'I was worried about the impact on Birmingham as a city,' he said. 'I was – at the time – the leader of the Liberal Democrat Group on the City Council and the economic damage to Birmingham would have been substantial.'

But it took Hemming's analysis of the situation for other investors to start to believe that an alternative to the Alchemy bid was even an option.

'I explained to those present that BMW were willing to give a dowry – something they were not aware of,' he said. 'Without that [the Phoenix Venture Holdings bid] would not have been possible.'

He recalls how it was impossible to quantify the potential damage a collapse of Rover in 2000 may have had, but that he, Carl Chinn and the unions all saw the saviour of Rover as a volume manufacturer as essential to avoid a massive local impact.

'It is difficult to quantify what that would have been but clearly many people would have lost their jobs in the supply chain. I do think it would have been harder hitting [than it was in 2005] simply because businesses were unprepared and had not had any opportunity to diversify.'

'The main thing was creating an alternative proposal in the first instance. A lot of the broad financial proposal came from me. It should be noted that I have been in business on my own since 1983 and more successfully than many of those who pushed me out of the deal.'

'The original Phoenix Consortium included Lord Mike Whitby [not then a Baron], Carl Chinn and myself. I think had John Towers not pushed us out of the arrangement there were many things that could have been done which would have made it more likely to get long-term financial success, but not all

Above left: John Hemming.

Above right: Carl Chinn, social historian.

of them were in it for Rover. That said, I have no doubt at all that of them all, John Edwards was motivated by a desire to save the company.'

Many contemporary news reports suggested that dealing with BMW was one of the biggest challenges during the takeover, but Hemming is adamant this is not true.

'I found them quite reasonable,' he said. 'Although I later handed over the negotiations to John Towers, which in retrospect was a mistake. I should not have trusted him. Towers did not appear to understand some of their objectives.'

Indeed, Hemming still believes that the events of 2000 and the way in which he, Carl Chinn and Mike Whitby were pushed out of what ultimately became Phoenix Venture Holdings may well have been instrumental in the company's eventual demise five years later.

'It is difficult to say what might have happened had the Phoenix Four not pushed the other consortium members out of the deal,' he said. 'I did think of issuing proceedings about this, but it would have derailed the bid at the time and that would have had a massive impact on the community.

'People should not forget that I am a high-tech entrepreneur with a record of success as well as a politician. Mike Whitby has also run a business. Pushing us out made it less likely to be a success.'

Calling All Cars – The MG Z Cars Are Born

It's no coincidence that the first images of the new MG range (codenamed X10, X20 and X30) were released in January 2001. At the time, much of the motor industry had its eyes focused on Detroit, where at the North American International Auto Show the wraps were coming off the BMW-built MINI.

The new MGs, meanwhile, were still in development, but MG Rover Group was keen to point out that MINI wasn't the only UK-based brand with a story to tell. After all, the MG Z cars had been developed by largely the same team of engineers and were arguably even more critical to the future of the British car industry – or at least that was the perception at the time.

Certainly that showed in the media. MG Rover's scattergun press release drummed up as many column inches as MINI's multi-million-pound Detroit reveal, certainly in the UK media, proving that the MG Rover saga was still well and truly in the public interest. It was the first move in what would come to be regarded as a highly strategic and at times inspirational marketing plan from MG Rover Group, which had little to no money to put behind it, but was free from the shackles of a large corporation – meaning it could afford to be quick, cheeky and bold with its advertising and PR rather than get bogged down in tiresome approvals.

At the same time, the first car to be put into production by MG Rover came along and it was a cracker. The Rover 75 Tourer was developed alongside the saloon while BMW still had feet under the boardroom table and was canned because it represented too much of a threat to the German firm's own cars,

14

The first ever image of the new MG range, released in January 2001.

The X10.

The X20.

The X30.

but with all the development and engineering pretty much complete, MG Rover was able to put it into production in a very short time frame.

The 75 Tourer was just what MG Rover needed, as not only did it generate some good coverage of its own, it also gave senior management the opportunity to talk about the upcoming new model range to the media attending the press launch. It was obvious, of course, that the new MGs were based on the Rover 25, 45 and 75, but it was critical that MG Rover positioned them correctly, as not just revised versions of relatively old models, but as thoroughly redesigned cars with stand-alone appeal.

Indeed, a lot of the chassis development for the Zeds had already been done. BMW may have stood in the way of Rover making its cars too dynamically competent, but that didn't stop the engineering teams from developing chassis revisions in secret, so the formula for sharpening up the cars' dynamics was already known.

Phoenix brought in two key people to help develop the new range. Rob Oldaker, a former Rover engineer himself, as head of engineering and Peter Stevens as director of design. The latter was known for designing the McLaren F1 and Lotus Esprit, so brought with him some fine pedigree as well.

By March 2001, MG Rover was ready to reveal the cars in the metal. The MG ZR, ZS and ZT made their debuts at the 2001 Geneva Motor Show, an event that was dominated by British brands as it also saw the Jaguar X-Type and all-new Range Rover put in their first public appearances. And while the Jaguar and Range Rover were clearly more advanced, it was the new MGs that got the

The Rover 75 Tourer.

most media coverage – the soap opera of 12 months prior obviously drawing in the attentions of the world's motoring scribes.

The entry-level car was the ZR, based on the 25 hatchback. It was the easiest of the three to develop as it used a body kit that was already in design when Rover Group was sold and the steering and suspension set-up from the VVC-engined Rover 25 GTi, which was a subtly excellent warm hatch. It was available in four different guises – 1.4, 1.8, 1.8 VVC and 2.0-litre turbo diesel form.

Next up was the 45-based ZS, which was the most incongruous fit in the range given that the Rover 45 it was based upon was never offered in sporting format at all and it had a rather dowdy, old-fashioned image. But with an aggressive body kit, arch-filling alloy wheels and the promise of 180PS in the range-topping 2.5-litre V6, it was an intriguing proposition. Lesser models came with a 1.8 petrol or 2.0 TD engine, both shared with the ZR.

Finally, there was the ZT – initially offered only as a V6 with either 160 or 190PS, though the range would be developed further down the line to include diesels and four-cylinder petrol models, along with a ZT-T estate car variant announced at the same time, but scheduled for production from September 2001.

The other Z Cars, meanwhile, would go on sale in June – and over the next three months MG Rover worked hard on its messaging to ensure that the Zeds

The MG Rover model range, as of September 2001.

would have as good a start in life as they could, including the announcement of a full-on motorsport plan, Nick Stephenson's links with Lola seeing a glorious return to Le Mans, as well as a rally career for the ZR and a British Touring Car Championship debut for the ZS. It was quite clear that whatever limited investment MG Rover had, it would be going into building the brand – something that was deemed essential in order to draw in external investment and keep MG Rover alive.

But would these three critically important cars be enough to save MG Rover?

Designed to Succeed – Peter Stevens's Part in the Z Car Story

One of the most significant moves in the formation of the new MG Rover Group was to bring in Peter Stevens as director of design.

Stevens was (and still is) one of the UK's most revered car designers, having been in charge of styling for the McLaren F1 and 1988 Lotus Esprit and M100 Elan.

Bringing him to MG Rover was considered a bit of a coup, though in reality he'd been consulting for the firm for some time before that.

'The decision to produce three MG versions of the Rover model range was made right at the start of the Towers, Stephenson, Beale and Edwards [Phoenix] period, around July 2000,' he said. 'I was invited to join as Director of Design, or 'Styling' as some engineers like to call the design department.

'The new tooling investment would be very low since all the Rover tools came with the purchase of the company from Rover. At the time of the acquisition

Peter Stevens (left) with Rover art cars in 2004.

MG Rover had no design studio of its own [and it] inherited a complex web of contracts with a number of local design consultancies – left over from a strange set of relationships set up by the previous management.

'Initially I chose to use RDS in Southam and Design Q in Coventry. At first it was just me doing all the design work but I then took on a young designer, Peter Andrews, from RDS, who had worked on the Rover 200 BRM and was then working on a body kit for the 200 that RDS planned to market themselves.

'We further developed this for the MG ZR as the first Z car. Senior management, particularly Nick Stephenson and John Edwards, quickly became good friends and received all my ideas with great enthusiasm – time was too short to fiddle about so Kevin Howe [the then managing director of MG Rover] was only shown full-size models when we were happy with them.'

Of the Z cars designed by his in-house team, it was the ZT of which Stevens was most proud.

'The little ZR was the best-selling Z car but was in fact a bit too fussy, being a mixture of my thoughts and those already decided, or tooled, by RDS. The ZS was a bit too long in the tooth, being derived from a Honda; it looked OK and had very nice aerodynamics – also developed by me – and in 180 form was great to drive and sounded very sporty.

Stevens today, still consulting on car design.

'But the ZT, particularly in wagon form, was probably the best resolved of the three; a good aerodynamic balance was achieved with a drag coefficient that was lower than all its competitors, CD 0.32.'

But while Stevens was proud of what his team had achieved, there were multiple frustrations along the way.

'There was not enough money for new head and tail lights,' he said. 'We had to be very clever with using Rover parts.

'One particular frustration [was] not being able to give the ZT round white on black instruments. The oval dials were fine for the 75 but looked wrong for the MG. And Kevin Howe, in his wisdom and as part of his cost-saving obsession, had the badges made cheaply in Turkey.

'Even before the company fell over they were fading in an alarming way and quickly looked cheap. I constantly argued that the badges are the most important details on a car; they are a prospective customer's first introduction to the car.'

Yet despite the challenges, Stevens recalls a positive atmosphere for most of the period between 2000 and 2005.

'In design it was great,' he added. 'I eventually set up a design studio at RDS with a really good team of young designers whose "culture" was modern, lively and fun. They were a pleasure to work with – the Rover Streetwise was a good, quick, modern project that everybody felt good about. The idea came from Design and was loved by the Phoenix guys. The Rover 75 Countryman was going to be even better but it never came to fruition.'

The ZR – How a 'Posh Supermini' Became a Cult Car among Youths

It was in many ways the least developed of the Z Cars, certainly in terms of its engineering, but the ZR (or X30) was a remarkably successful car given the background behind its development.

Under the skin, it was essentially a Rover 25 GTi but with slightly firmer dampers. Essentially, the 25 was a pretty decent car to drive and that weighed in the ZR's favour, especially with the MG/25 GTi's faster steering rack. On an open and twisty road, it could do very well indeed, while its performance was comparably better than many of its rivals.

There were four powertrain choices. At the entry level, there was the ZR 105, which came with the 1.4-litre 16v Rover K-Series – an eager and lively unit with 103PS, which was a far greater power output than similar-sized 1.4s from other manufacturers. Next up was the ZR 120, with a 118PS 1.8-litre unit, followed by the VVC, which had variable valve timing. The VVC engine had previously been used in the 25 GTi and MGF, but in the ZR it was breathed upon further to bring its total power output up from 142PS to 160PS, enough for it to do 0–60 mph in 7.4 seconds.

For those seeking frugal fun there was also a ZR TD, which may have only had 101PS but thanks to low gearing and eager torque delivery was surprisingly willing – indeed, between 30–50 and 50–70 mph in fourth gear, it would outpace the ZR 160.

ZR was previewed as the X30 in January 2001.

Rover 25 GTi was the precursor to the ZR.

The ZR 160 was still the pick of the bunch, though – the variable valve-timed engine delivering most of its power at the top of its rev range, encouraging enthusiastic driving. The rev-hungry nature of the engine made it feel quicker than it looked on paper, too, and while cars such as the Honda Civic Type 'R' and Ford Focus ST170 were better cars overall, they couldn't match the MG for value for money, which was its trump card across the model range. Indeed, only the diesel model looked less than a complete bargain – the rest of the range was priced hugely competitively in order to bring in new customers.

All of which was a far cry from the demure 'Middle England' image that the 25 on which it was based exuded. Introduced in December 1999, the 25 was an evolution of the 'R3' 200 and was a pleasant if slightly drab supermini, popular with older motorists who were loyal to the Rover brand, but with little in the way of image to attract younger drivers. Sure, it was quite good fun to drive, but the chrome grille and wood-adorned interior were anachronisms that youthful buyers simply didn't want.

What the ZR achieved, then, was incredible – for within less than a year of going on sale, the little MG had become something of a cult car among younger motorists.

Part of this was down to the 'Citroen Saxo-effect' – by fitting sporty adornments to moderately powered examples of its supermini range, the French manufacturer had created – in the Saxo VTR – a car that was cool to look at,

ZR 160 was top of the range.

Younger motorists liked the low running costs of 1.4-litre ZR 105.

cool to be seen in and visually identical to its more powerful twin, the VTS. The ZR was more of the same – you could buy a three-door ZR 105, upgrade from the standard 16-inch wheels to the larger 17s and it would look outwardly no different to the VVC-powered ZR 160. Go for one of the hero colours – Trophy Yellow, Trophy Blue or Solar Red – and you had a car that was vibrant to look at, too.

A bargain-basement entry model – just £9,995 on the road – added even further appeal. With some dealer-enhanced insurance packages and affordable monthly payments, younger drivers could be behind the wheel of a cultish new MG for the same monthly instalment as they'd pay for insurance alone on a clapped-out Ford Escort.

It was a heavily incentivised practice, with MG Rover and its dealers both contributing towards a number of insurance-led finance deals, but it got bums on seats. And young bums at that – these were the family car and fleet customers of the future, and getting them into the MG brand below the age of 24 was a major part of MG Rover's future growth plan, as it not only revamped the image of the company from that of an 'old person's car brand' to a much more youthful one, but it also brought in the people that would help make MG Rover more saleable when it came to seek external investment.

The interior was outdated compared to rivals.

A ZR 160 in Monogram Biomorphic Green.

Whatever would happen next as the MG Rover story neared its final throes, there's no denying that, with the ZR, the company created the right car at the right time. Indeed, by the end of 2002, it had become MG Rover's best-selling model outright and was just outside the UK's top ten seller lists – for an outdated car developed on a shoestring budget, it was evidence that the ZR was a marketing master stroke.

The ZS – How an Old Dog Learned New Tricks

If there was one car within the MG portfolio that raised more than its fair share of eyebrows, it was the ZS.

On paper, the model codenamed X20 was the least appealing of all the Z cars. It was based on the Rover 45 – a car that was as ordinary as a car could be.

Competent and good to drive, but lacking in any sense of spirit or occasion, the 45 was introduced in 2000 and was based on the 1994 Rover 400, which in turn was based on the 1991 Honda Domani.

So when the ZS debuted, what MG Rover's engineers were working with was a ten-year-old design, based on a car that never really set the world on fire in the first place.

Yet beneath its tweedy exterior, the 45 was an engineer's dream thanks to its fully independent suspension – something that MG Rover's engineering chief, Rob Oldaker, was quite open about at the Z car media launch.

The X20 prototype, which became the ZS.

26

'The ZS, you could argue, has suspension elements that are arguably the best of the three because it is double-wishbone all-round,' he said. 'Therefore some of the things that are quite difficult to do when putting more torque through the front wheels of a strut-suspension car are not there on that car. So [it] had a natural composure and lack of steering corruption.

'Then there's the amount of grip that's available on dry roads. That was probably the most illuminating thing for me.'

The ZS had another ace up its sleeve, too, in the form of its KV6 engine – a happy hangover from Rover's decision to replace the four-cylinder Rover 420 GSi with the 2.0-litre version of the Rover 75's KV6 back in 2000. The block for the 150PS 2.0-litre unit was no bigger than that of the 2.5-litre unit from the range-topping 75s, which had a power output of 177PS, and thanks to the re-engineering of the 45 engine bay for the V6 flagship, it meant that the larger-capacity engine would drop straight in.

In the ZS, that was an astonishing amount of power for such a small car, but thanks to the wizardry of MG's engineers, led by Oldaker, the platform was more than capable of handling the power. Not only that, but the steering refinements carried out during racetrack testing (much of the development work on the Z cars was done at Pembrey Circuit) meant it had an extremely sharp and accurate turn-in.

What MG's engineers had done, essentially, was take Honda's basics and transform them into a chassis that was developed as far as it could go – something that would not only give the ZS some success in motorsport, but which would raise one or two eyebrows elsewhere as well.

As well as the V6, dubbed the ZS 180, there was a lesser petrol-engined variant, the 118PS ZS 120, along with a 101PS diesel known as the ZS TD. The diesel was

The interior was
based on Rover 45.

A large rear spoiler gave an extreme appearance when on a saloon.

the weakest link, with the extra weight of the engine having an impact on both performance and handling balance, yet it was still dynamically superior to many of its rivals.

The 1.8, meanwhile, may have lacked the drama of the KV6, but it was arguably the most rewarding of the lot. With less weight upfront, it had a sharper turn-in and better chassis balance, which led many people to question why there was never a ZS with the 160PS VVC engine found in the ZR and TF.

The answer is simply one of range rationalisation. To offer the V6 flagship at an affordable price point (£21,995) there simply wasn't a big enough gap between the ZS 120 and the ZS 180 for it to fit. Depending on who you believe, the ZS 160 was frequently put forward in internal meetings only to be snubbed by senior management.

Irrespective, back in June 2001 it wasn't a question on many people's lips. Instead, talk at the media launch of the Z cars was how, somehow, it was the ZS that was the pick of the bunch.

In Trophy Blue and with a large wing spoiler on the boot, a saloon version of the ZS looked like it was trying hard to be a Subaru Impreza WRX – something that's not as uncanny as you'd imagine, for it was Peter Stevens Design that had consulted with Subaru all through the WRX's gestation, from road car to aerodynamically optimised rally machine. The ZS was from the same pen and featured a similar aerodynamic profile – that rear wing was for more than just show.

Hatchbacks looked more subtle.

It wasn't just the styling that had a hint of Impreza about it, either – indeed, *EVO*, the car enthusiasts' magazine, described the ZS as a 'cut-price' WRX, while *Autocar* said it was 'the finest-handling front-wheel-drive car on the market right now'.

This was not faint praise – jingoistic loyalty in the automotive media had long since become a thing of the past, so the reasons for the ZS being declared such a great driver's car were based on merit rather than patriotic allegiance.

Even BBC's *Top Gear* liked it, with former racing driver cum TV presenter Tiff Needell saying 'To get a car that's this quick, this much fun and that handles so well anywhere else will cost you a lot more money ... it really is that good.'

The ZS, then, got off to a great start, but it wasn't enough to disguise the fact that some of the car was woefully outdated. It may have looked pretty cool, but the mid-size MG still made do with a harsh and plasticky cabin that was an ergonomic nightmare and for which the company still had to pay a licensing fee to Honda. Whenever it was group tested alongside its contemporaries, the MG was slated for its ancient cabin, nasty aftermarket radio and lack of cabin storage, while elements such as a cupholder that slotted into the central armrest and a switch for the passenger window that was next to the handbrake for both the driver and passenger to use seemed both cheap and nasty.

Those who loved the ZS adored it for its charms and its immense appeal as a driver's car. But to get that far, it needed showroom appeal and the cabin layout simply didn't help.

In 2003, a new entry-level ZS appeared – the ZS 110, with wind-down windows and a 1.6-litre engine along with a £10,995 price tag as a lead-in

A ZS 180 in XPower Grey.

The ZS 110.

showroom special, and for the price of other manufacturers' superminis, or a direct rival to a Proton Wira or a Kia Shuma, it made sense, not least because it was well-equipped and fun to drive. But this was also indicative of MG Rover being forced to cheapen its brand to chase volume at all costs.

For a car that the cognoscenti knew was one of the best drivers' cars that not a lot of money could buy, it was a rather ignominious position for the British Touring Car Championship race-winning ZS to find itself in and a barometer of MG Rover's by-now parlous financial position. But for a short period of time, the ZS truly represented the best of British and a well-sorted early car is now a deserved collectors' item.

The ZT – When Jekyll Met Hyde

The demure and civilised nature of the Rover 75 made it one of the most pleasant family cars on the road, but also the most difficult of the MG trio to convert into a performance saloon.

It wasn't that the chassis wasn't up to it: far from it, in fact, as the 75 was actually very well balanced and quite rewarding to hustle along. But the nature of the car was one of serene comfort, not snarling performance.

Of the three Z cars, then, the 'X10' was the one with the biggest personality crisis.

It was also the toughest one to market. Whereas the ZR and ZS offered performance on a budget, the bigger ZT was competing against much more expensive metal including the likes of the BMW 3-Series – one of the reasons

The X10 concept.

why the idea of an MG-badged 75 was stillborn in the first place was it wouldn't compromise BMW's sales.

The challenge for MG was getting it right, and it was the model that Peter Stevens spent most of his personal time on, though it's a little-known fact that the MG grille on the ZT was designed by none other than Harris Mann, famous for designing the Triumph TR7 and Austin Allegro.

Amazingly, Stevens and his team managed to completely transform the image of Richard Woolley's original, rather delicate, 75 design – a tough challenge given the car had lots of chrome detailing around the door bottoms and waistline.

One area that helped was with the wheels – standard 75 wheels were a mere 15 inches and as a result it was easy to make the ZT look beefier, with a choice of 18-inch rims that gave the car a much more purposeful stance. The track was wider, too, while fat 225-section tyres promised plenty of grip.

The interior also needed to be completely redesigned as the gentlemen's club cabin of the 75 was nowhere near sporty enough for a performance saloon. The comfort seats – both velour and leather – were cast aside in favour of either 'Matrix' or 'Monaco' seat trim, the former consisting of chequered cloth inserts and imitation leather bolsters, with the latter being a more hard-wearing and thickly padded sports seat. Colour-coded carpets and metallic-finish dash inserts

A ZT 190, the flagship of the range.

The cabin was quite different to the 75 on which it was based.

replaced the traditional wood finish found in the 75, while the 75's rather flat and uninspiring steering wheel was replaced with a chunkier leather-clad wheel with MG central boss. Considering it was based on the same architecture, the ZT's cabin looked notably different from that of the car on which it was based.

It helped with the car's premium image that, unlike the other Z cars, the ZT was only offered in one standard trim level, with a choice of two V6 petrol engines. The flagship powerplant was the 190PS 2.5-litre unit in the ZT 190, which used the 177PS engine from the Rover 75 but with different camshafts, a wider throttle body and a larger air intake. That was sufficient to give it a 0–60 time of 7.7 seconds and a top speed of 140 mph, though it was the ZT's in-gear acceleration that was most impressive thanks to the low-down torque and responsiveness of the quad cam KV6.

The lesser model was no slouch, either. The ZT 160 used a 160PS version of the KV6, detuned from the 177PS unit found in the Rover 75 via ECU software – and easily turned back up again, as many an aftermarket tuner would go on to prove. Indeed, the only reason why the ZT 160 was detuned was to leave a big enough gap in performance between it and the 190, helping to drive sales towards the more expensive flagship car. The 160 did 0–60 mph in 8.8 seconds, with a top speed of 127 mph.

It was worth the extra, too. The additional performance, seductive exhaust note and 'Monaco' leather-bolstered sports seats gave it a genuine muscle car feel, while the aggressive frontal styling and chunky rear spoiler added further to its Jekyll and Hyde persona.

'The ZT has what I call Outside Lane Credibility,' said Peter Stevens. 'I get a kick out of that. There's no doubt, if you're in a position to be overtaken, that it looks great when it's passing you.'

33

Two rear spoilers were available. This was the most extreme.

At the time of the ZT's launch, MG also released pictures of the ZT-T – an estate version of the MG based on the new Rover 75 Tourer, though this would not be put into production until the autumn of 2001.

As well as the styling differences between the ZT and 75, Rod Oldaker's team went to great lengths to change the way the car felt from the driver's seat. The steering was heavier and faster, while the gear shift was shorter and had a weightier feel to it.

But it was on fast-flowing A-roads where it really came alive, with great mid-range acceleration and an agile chassis that managed to combine impressive handling with a level of comfort not normally found on a high-performance saloon – it was certainly a more supple car to drive than any BMW or Audi of the period, while the only front-wheel-drive car of a similar size to match it for steering and handling prowess was the Alfa Romeo 156.

The decision to launch the ZT in V6 flavour only was taken because MG Rover Group deemed it essential to position the biggest MG model as a muscle car icon, and also to make it something for buyers of other Z cars to aspire to, but it was always the company's intention to expand the line-up later on.

Autumn 2001 also saw the arrival of diesel versions of the ZT, which lacked the outright performance of the V6-engined models but were essential to put the ZT on fleet user-chooser lists. Both were badged as CDTi but there were two power outputs – 115 and 131PS – with the key difference between the two being a simple software reflash. Again, it's no surprise that modifications are common.

The ZT excelled dynamically.

The ZT 120 was a new entry-level model.

In 2003, a four-cylinder petrol ZT arrived in two different formats. The entry-level car was a normally aspirated 1.8-litre K-Series using the same engine as the base model Rover 75 and, much like the ZS 110, was a price-point model designed to make the MG Z cars accessible to customers on a smaller budget. It developed 118PS and was never more than an average performer, but was nevertheless still quite a fun car to drive as it benefitted from the chassis and steering improvements of other ZT models.

Indeed, there were few cars on the market with a £15,000 asking price that were as much fun to drive – the ZT was priced to compete with the entry-spec Ford Mondeo and Vauxhall Vectra, but was a much more compelling proposition.

The 1.8 was identifiable from other models by its smaller 17-inch alloys but equipment levels were largely the same, although climate control was never an option and it got the cheaper CD30 front-loading CD player rather than the premium flip-front system fitted to posher ZTs, though by this time the stereos were nowhere near as good as the original BMW-derived systems, a side-effect of MG Rover Group's 'Project Drive' rationalisation programme covered more fully later in this book.

The second application of the 1.8 K-Series was somewhat more interesting and replaced the ZT 160 V6 in the line-up, yet retained the ZT 160 name. Under the bonnet was a turbocharged version of the 16-valve 1.8 K-Series developing 159PS

The ZT 160 1.8T appeared in 2003, replacing the V6.

A ZT Sports Auto.

and offering faster performance than the detuned V6 – 0–60 mph in 8.1 seconds and a top speed of 137 mph. The 1.8T was, at the time, arguably the pick of the range – less than £20,000 for the saloon and £1,500 extra for the ZT-T, yet almost as quick as the range-topping 190 V6.

Sadly, by 2003 MG Rover Group sales were struggling, and while the ZT and 75 remained fine cars, the rationalisation brought on by Project Drive was starting to show and the later ZTs never felt as composed, well-finished or refined as the early models.

Nevertheless, the ZT achieved what it needed to, bringing the MG model range into areas of the market where Rover could never have previously competed. Whatever was happening at a corporate level, the designers, engineers and marketers did their absolute best – the ZT was every inch the proof of that, and is already establishing itself as a collectable sports saloon.

The ZT-T – Loads of Fun

Although MG's approach to the market was based around three models at the time of the cars' June 2001 debut, the ZT-T (for Tourer) was always part of the plan, to the extent that it appeared in the launch brochure billed as a 'forthcoming attraction' and was first shown as a concept, subbed X11.

Indeed, the ZT-T was Peter Stevens's favourite Z car variant, both in terms of its design and its aerodynamic performance, which he said was easier to work with than any of the other Zeds. That's why the ZT-T was chosen as MG's Bonneville Land Speed Record car, a rather unusual pursuit for what was essentially a compact executive estate car.

The MG X11 Concept.

The ZT-T in launch 190 specification.

MG made up one ZT-T in Trophy Blue for sales and marketing purposes, but its primary focus was on launching the mainstream variants of the ZR, ZS and ZT first. The ZT-T finally arrived in showrooms in September 2001, concurrent with the other car in MG Rover's 'next phase' of new products – the TF sports car, which replaced the MGF.

By the end of its first full year of trading, the company could rightfully claim that it had launched six all-new cars (75 Tourer, ZR, ZS, ZT, ZT-T and TF)

The ZT-T was just as practical as the 75 Tourer.

while also surpassing its 250,000 manufacturing target by 10,000 units – a bold message to send out to the industry and one that was central to the ZT-T media launch as MG Rover Group began its quest for external investment.

It was also an opportunity for MG to talk about how it perceived the ZT-T to be unique in the market – and to a certain degree they had a point. Yes, there were other estate cars with sporting pretensions, but none quite so overt as the MG. Models such as M-Sport variants of the BMW 3-Series and S-Line Audis were largely just trim levels, whereas the ZT-T was a sports estate in its own right – and a good one at that.

Mechanically it was identical to the saloon, and although it carried a little extra weight, which increased the 0–60 time by half a second, it was by no means lagging behind it dynamically. It was also hugely practical, with over 1,200 litres of usable boot space with the split-fold seat fully retracted and a handy split tailgate, which allowed the glass area to lift up separately from the rest of the load door for smaller items.

MG marketed the ZT-T at families with 'active lifestyles', as was very much the industry marketing fad at the time, but it was the fleet market that was central to its volume appeal and within weeks of the flagship V6 models appearing there were tax-efficient diesels joining the range, too. As per the V6s, these were

Above, below and opposite above: A fleet of ZT-Ts were used as fast-response vehicles by the West Midlands Ambulance Service, as well as the police.

Diesel accounted for a large amount of sales.

mechanically identical to the saloons, but whereas the saloon sales volume was split 65:35 in favour of petrol engines, the station wagon volumes were the other way round, indicative of its appeal to the company car market.

Indeed, fleet sales were an essential part of the ZT-T's marketing plan post-Project Drive and the 2003 model year, too, and not just with diesels. The 1.8 petrol ZT-T 120 joined the fray as an entry-level variant in 2003, with a sub £16,500 price tag. It wasn't brilliant on emissions compared to some more modern rival manufacturers' engines, but the low purchase price and decent standard equipment made it an appealing prospect providing you weren't seeking out-and-out performance.

At the same time as the ZT-T 120's debut, the ZT-T 160 was also replaced, the low-power V6 being usurped by a 1.8 Turbo K-Series, as per the saloon line-up, though the turbo engine in the estate was never a huge seller.

Nevertheless, the ZT-T was a compelling companion to the other Z cars and accounted for around 25 per cent of total ZT sales.

The ZT-T 120, a new entry-level model for 2003.

The ZT 160 1.8
Turbo engine.

The ZT 260 – The Pure-bred Muscle Car

In 2003, MG Rover Group was really starting to struggle, but with very limited funds in the coffers it had to diversify in order to showcase engineering expertise that would convince external investors it had the talent and diversity to succeed.

Thanks to Nick Stephenson's Lola connections, the company entered into an agreement to take over the rights to the Qvale Mangusta supercar – an unusual addition to the roster of a struggling marque, but one that was seen as a flagbearer for the MG XPower division, the sports and racing arm that was also seen as a potential sports car offshoot.

The marriage also created an unusual offspring in the form of the ZT 260 – an MG ZT equipped with the 4.6-litre V8 engine from the Ford Mustang. There was also a V8-engined Rover 75, but this was even more of a niche.

Initial development of the car was outsourced to Prodrive, but was brought back in-house after a fallout between the two companies around the cost of delivering the project and what Prodrive saw as unsurmountable engineering challenges, yet the in-house team finally delivered it a year after the first prototype was exhibited.

Creating a V8-powered rear-drive sports saloon out of the Rover 75 wasn't the most obvious idea for a company that was fighting for survival, but as an engineering exercise it was both fascinating and surprisingly complex, as the longitudinally mounted V8 would only work with a rear-wheel-drive set-up, so in order to make it function MG Rover's engineers got rid of the spare wheel well to make way for the V8's rear diff and substantially revised the floor plan and bulkhead to accommodate the propshaft and gearbox bellhousing.

It came with an all-new six-mount rear subframe with multi-link rear suspension, while power was distributed through a limited slip differential to

The ZT 260 in saloon form.

The Mustang V8 was made to fit, but installation wasn't straightforward.

Above and below: The front end looked little different, save for a different grille. The biggest changes were at the rear and hidden from sight.

ensure predictable and tractable power delivery. Uprated brakes and meatier steering completed the package.

In terms of raw power, the V8's 260PS wasn't huge – indeed, Japanese manufacturers of the era were squeezing much more out of 2.0-litre turbocharged petrols. But to compare the ZT 260 to such cars was to do it a disservice, as this was a muscle car in the traditional mould. It wasn't so much about out-and-out performance (though 0–60 mph in 6.2 seconds was decent enough) so much as the raw experience of an old-school muscle car, with a seductive V8 soundtrack, incredible torque and rear-wheel drive.

It was brilliantly executed, too. Yes, the fit and finish was a bit half-hearted in places – under the bonnet, for example, you could still clearly see the Mustang logo on the rocker covers, but it was exquisitely engineered beneath the skin and that showed in the way it drove.

It was a truly remarkable car, especially given MG's limited development budget compared to rivals. In hard corners it delivered limpet-like grip, the brakes were incredible and the steering heavy but wonderfully precise, with none of the torque steer encountered on front-wheel-drive ZTs.

With a peak torque figure of 410Nm at 4,000 rpm and a soundtrack that was utterly beguiling, the ZT 260 was not only rewarding to drive, but exciting, too. The five-speed manual gearbox was its weakest link, with an overly

Above and opposite above: The 260 was also offered as an estate.

46

Above and overleaf above: The ZT 260 was more commonly seen in facelift form.

mechanical feel, while the revised bellhousing meant there was nowhere to rest your clutch foot between changes, but a quick blast down a country lane was enough for you to forgive its vices. It may have been strictly for enthusiasts, but the 260 was nevertheless a wonderful car.

Around 800 were made, of which around 200 were estates. Today, they're rare and already highly collectable – an oddball but wonderful car and an intriguing flagship that showed that, even in times of austerity, MG Rover's engineers were among the best in the world.

ZT XPower 385 – The ZT That Never Was

When the original ZT 260 was announced, MG Rover planned to produce two variants: the standard 260 and a supercar-baiting XPower 385 model, which was to be hand-finished by XPower Sport and Racing and would come with a Roush supercharger.

The two were announced concurrently, and at least two working prototypes were produced – one saloon and one estate. But when MG Sports and Racing went into administration ahead of MG Rover Group, development was halted.

It was said by internal sources to have been almost ready for production, but the need for better brakes and a wider track to manage the extra power was too expensive for further development. It was a wonderful might-have-been and could have been a glorious hero car for the MG Z range, but realistically was never more than an extremely low-volume prospect that would have cost more to develop than it would have generated in sales.

Above and below: The ZT XPower 385.

To mark the launch of the ZT 260 and to further demonstrate its engineering skills, MG Rover Group pulled of an unusual PR stunt in 2003 to raise awareness of the ZT-T, which was its most profitable mainstream model.

The aim was to get itself in the *Guinness Book of World Records* for the World's Fastest Estate Car, and to achieve this it took itself off to the famous Bonneville salt flats in Utah, USA, to compete in the annual Speed Week Nationals.

In some respects, this seemed a bit of a jolly for senior management – Nick Stephenson was himself a hobby drag racer and design chief Peter Stevens was a huge fan of the sport. It was certainly a project on which Stevens and Stephenson closely collaborated, with Stevens placing a huge focus on the car's aerodynamic efficiency, helped by the ZT-T's naturally low drag co-efficient of 0.32 cd.

The reasoning behind the project, codenamed X-15, was to not only exploit the new V8-engined 'halo cars' of the Z line-up, but to also celebrate an oft-overlooked part of MG's history, as the brand had set a number of previous Bonneville records going back to 1951. It also gave MG the opportunity to carry out strategic development work on the 385PS version of the V8, which was scheduled to go into both the ZT and the XPower SV supercar, derived from the Qvale Mangusta.

MG achieved its aim, too, with the ZT-T entering the record books with a top speed of 225.609 mph, an achievement that still stands as a world record.

'This is not just about setting world records, this is about testing MG's vehicles to their limits, in some of the most extreme conditions you can find

The Bonneville car wows the crowds at the 2004 Farnborough Air Show.

The salt flats are demanding, but ZT-T was properly prepared.

Bonneville veteran Pat Kinne was drafted in to drive the car.

in the world,' said Peter Stevens at the time. 'The added challenges of meeting strict technical and safety regulations which are set by the Southern California Timing Association make our achievement of 225.609 mph with a virtually stock MG ZT-T all the more satisfying.'

MG's land speed racing roots went back to the early 1930s and its Bonneville roots back to 1951 when Lt Col A.T. 'Goldie' Gardner ran a streamliner powered by a crank-driven supercharged production 1250cc 4-cylinder MG TD engine. Goldie planned an assault on numerous records, both in a straight line and around a specially surfaced 10-mile circular course. Despite rain cutting short the attempts, at the end of the week he had accumulated a total of sixteen records with a fastest run slightly over 145 mph.

Famous names such as Stirling Moss and Phil Hill went on to set records driving for MG in the harsh and challenging environment of the Utah salt desert, where daily temperatures of more than 100 deg F/38 deg C, high altitude and low grip added further challenges.

The project began in 2002, when MG Rover approached the California-based So-Cal Speed Shop to build and run the car. Custom car specialists So-Cal were professional land speed racers, well known for their Bonneville achievements in the late forties and early fifties.

Roush Performance was chosen for the powertrain development and delivered a bored-out 6.0-litre version of the Ford V8 with electronic fuel injection that developed 765PS without the aid of an intercooler, let alone a supercharger or turbo. More than enough, it was felt, to propel the ZT-T to its goal of 200 mph.

On its very first official 'shakedown' pass the ZT-T ran 164 mph. The following month, now with sponsorship from Mobil 1, the car made a licensing pass at 181.521 mph.

New vehicles which are running for the first time at Bonneville are required to run on the short course at a speed of more than 175 mph, before being allowed to run on the long course where speeds are measured at 3-, 4- and 5-mile markers as well as the terminal speed.

A further 2 miles are available for slowing the cars. Cars running at over 185 mph are required to fit speed-reducing parachutes. The chutes safely slow the cars in a stable manner to around 100 mph after which the brakes are used to stop at the 7-mile marker.

In August that year, the So-Cal Racing Team accompanied by Nick Stephenson, Peter Stevens, and the Roush crew made the 700-plus-mile trek to Bonneville where Bonneville veteran Pat Kinne clicked off a licensing pass of 207 mph on the Bonneville short course, backed up with a blistering 223 mph pass on the long course. Some minor pitch-attitude tweaking saw the ZT-T make a final run at 225.609 mph (306.9 km/h).

'Bonneville and record breaking is a very important part of MG history,' said Nick Stephenson. '225 mph with our ZT-T is part of our future, because it signals the direction for further high-performance models.'

Don't be fooled by the white stuff: conditions at Bonneville are intensely hot.

'We were completely thrilled,' said Peter Stevens. 'We had high hopes that the X-15 would perform as predicted, but in a competitive situation, exaggerated by the extremely harsh environment of Bonneville, you can never be certain. Not only are we tremendously pleased with the outright achievement, but that this form of extreme performance testing has demonstrated the capability of future powertrain and chassis developments.'

The Bonneville car remained in MG Rover Group's ownership and was sold in 2006 by the administrators' auctioneers Wyles Hardy, when it sold to an undisclosed buyer for just £13,700.

Z Car Atomix – Making MG Whole Again

Back in the early 2000s, there was one band that was gathering almost as many column inches as MG Rover Group itself – namely Atomic Kitten, a girl-power group that had more than its own fair share of internal wrangling, concluding with lead singer Kerry Katona leaving the band in 2001.

Like MG Rover, Atomic Kitten was undergoing something of a relaunch and – at the time of the 2002 British Motor Show – was once again sitting pretty at the top of the UK pop charts. It was quite a coup, then, for MG Rover to not only get the band to sponsor its ZS British Touring Car Championship racer, but also

MG ZR and ZS 'Atomix' with, Kittens Liz McClarnon and Jenny Frost.

to launch their own special edition range of Zed Cars, which were revealed on the press day of the NEC show with a live performance on the MG Rover stand.

Alongside three of their big hits, Atomic Kitten also revealed a new range of special edition ZRs and ZSs named 'Atomix', derived from the popular MG ZR+ 105 and MG ZS+ 120 models, featuring additional specification and available in Le Mans Green, Solar Red and an all-new colour called XPower Grey, as used on the MG Rally and Touring race cars.

The MG ZR Atomix SE came with side sill finishers, 16-inch 'Hairpin' alloy wheels and front fog lamps, with part-leather Monaco seats, a leather steering

Atomix models celebrated the band's sponsorship of XPower BTCC Cars.

Above and ovelaf above: The Kittens appeared on the MG Rover stand at the 2002 British International Motor Show.

XPower Grey Atomix models were aimed at a youth market.

wheel and a Kenwood CD player, along with electric sunroof and windows and remote central door locking. It was only available with the 1.4-litre engine and was priced at £12,395, targeted at both younger and female customers.

The ZS was based on the 1.8-litre 120+ and received similar treatment, along with standard air conditioning.

Speaking at the press conference, Atomic Kitten's Jenny Frost said: 'We've had a great time racing the MG ZS in the BTCC, winning six races in our class. And it's great to continue this, with the MG Atomix SE cars. We're so pleased to be associated with MG – it's a great British brand.'

However, in a separate interview with the author on the same day, when asked how she liked her new ZR, Frost replied: 'I don't know yet – I don't have a driving licence.'

Best laid plans and all...

Project Drive – A Different Kind of Asset Stripping

Throughout MG Rover Group's existence, there was a huge cost-saving exercise going on in the background.

'Project Drive' was implemented by the board to look at ways of saving money on the cost of producing each model without any noticeable detriment to the customer and involved lots of invisible (and a few more visible) changes in order to reduce the build cost of each car.

Sadly, in doing so the cars became compromised more so than the accountants behind the project ever realised.

The ZR, for example, had much of its soundproofing stripped out in 2002, including under-bonnet insulation and a number of trim clips. Tiny savings, but when applied to large volume production these represented big savings.

Little details disappeared, such as glovebox illumination, the trim strip on the dashboard and the chrome tip on the end of the exhaust, while other details were so small they seemed ridiculously stingy, like the removal of the sticker that pointed to the car's bonnet stay, or the printed label from the power steering reservoir.

The satin black door finishers were made body colour, twin horns were replaced by a single horn, the alloy wheel centre caps were downgraded from stainless steel to painted nickel and the carpet insulation was halved in thickness.

By the 2003 model the cuts were even more rife. The illumination around the ignition barrel disappeared, stereo head units were replaced by cheap Blaupunkt or Kenwood aftermarket units, the rear heater ducts were removed and the Union/Chequered flags disappeared from the tailgate and C-pillars.

The ZS, meanwhile, saw many of the above changes as well as losing its door trim finishers, driveshaft dampers, volumatic alarm sensor, rear seatbelt clip housings, heated door mirrors and rear grab handles.

The biggest shame, though, was the Project Drive effect on the ZT, which began to lose its premium appeal. Cheaper badges, ugly non-integrated stereos and removal of some of the nicer options such as the rear sun blind and twin

Post-PPD cars didn't look very different from the outside.

The under-bonnet soundproofing and badging disappeared.

The post-Project Drive ZS seen here has an aftermarket stereo and is missing internal door trims.

Above left and above right: The badge quality also deteriorated.

cupholders really pared down the fit and finish, while other changes such as thinner carpets and seat material also had a detrimental effect on the brand's flagship.

In time, other Project Drive issues started to surface – a key one being removal of underseal from certain parts of the car's underside, meaning that quite often the later MG Z cars succumbed to underbody corrosion much more quickly than the better-built earlier models. There was also a huge amount of variation from one car to the next, depending on how rigidly the factory workers applied

ZT models from 2003 onward were worst affected by Project Drive.

the cost-cutting changes – almost as if they were especially stingy when being watched over by management.

There's also a lack of consistency within model years, with some parts reappearing and others disappearing as time went by.

In some respects, MG got off lightly. The Project Drive changes to the company's Rover models, especially the 75, were far more visible and the interior trim of the 25 and 45 in particular was vastly inferior to the launch models.

But these were desperate times for MG Rover Group and a saving of just £1 on a car could represent a six-figure saving against overall production, which meant that towards the end the reduction in quality went from being almost invisible to hugely evident – some commentators even believe that Project Drive was one of the biggest contributors to MG Rover's eventual downfall, as the product quality had deteriorated so badly that it represented the company in a bad light.

Monogram Programme – The Personal Touch

With a need to diversify into further niches, MG Rover Group created the Monogram Programme for the 2003 model year, introduced in September 2002.

The scheme was similar to the 'Autobiography' range offered on Land Rover and Range Rover models during the Rover Group years and brought the already existing 'Personal Line' interiors together with a range of 'Chromescent',

Above and below: The author's MG ZT 190 in Spectre Chromactive.

'Chromactive' and 'Super Metallic' paint colours, which were factory-ordered to provide a unique finish.

The Chromescent colours were pearlescent paint with a chrome-flake finish to give a sparkly finish in bright light while the more advanced Chromactive colours, developed by paint maker DuPont, were created to 'flip' from one colour to another in different lights. The move resulted in some startling colours such as Typhoon, which switched between blue and green, and Spectre, which flipped between lilac purple and midnight blue depending on ambient light conditions. Even in low light conditions, the refractive nature of the paint caused the car to change colour from different angles, and while it was a gimmick, it was one that was surprisingly popular with customers.

A total of twenty different paint finishes were offered, from subtle hues such as Mirage (a sparkly pearlescent white with purple overtones) to some wilder shades such as Orange Grove, which featured flakes of both bright orange and bright yellow and certainly wasn't a hue for shrinking violets.

In addition to the exterior enhancements, Monogram specifications included 'Personal Line' leather in Copperbeech Red, Catkin Green or Neptune Blue, plus a range of brightly coloured Alcantara inserts, all hand-finished and built to a much higher quality standard than the mainstream interior materials.

The Monogram initiative also included a number of factory-fitted options. Hi-line Navigation systems, roof-mounted DVD players and more alloy wheel options were available for customers to individualise their cars.

At launch, John Sanders, MG Rover Group marketing director, said: 'The Monogram programme provides an exclusive opportunity for MG and Rover customers to realise their personality through automotive style.'

Some of the Monogram interior options weren't for shrinking violets!

Types of Paint Finishes
Monogram Chromactive

Chromactive paints were the most powerful colours of the twenty shades offered within the choice of Monogram hues. They were neither metallic nor pearlescent, yet gave a dramatic colour shift even in low light and had high levels of opacity and durability, and were a £2,100 option.

The paint formulation used DuPont's unique multi-layered 'ChromaFlair' pigment flakes, which gave a wide range of hues depending on the viewing angle and the angle of light incidence. Five ultra-thin layers of material were applied to an external carrier film to produce the effect of changing colours through the physics of light interference.

According to MG Rover's official press release, the composition of these layers 'produced colour effects similar to those found in nature, such as soap bubbles, butterfly wings and peacock feathers', but in reality they became a nightmare for bodyshop owners...

There were just two Chromactive colours – Spectre and Typhoon – with Typhoon (blue/green) being the most popular.

Monogram Chromescent

Chromescent colours also had a striking appearance, but with a less extreme colour movement than the Chromactives. A groundcoat of coloured undercoat between the primer and the final colour coat added depth to the colour and an impression of different colour layers. Three Chromescent colours were offered for Monogram – Mirage, Gulf Stream and Glacier. They were a £1,500 option.

An MG ZT in Monogram Moonshine, which replaced Mirage.

Monogram Super Metallics and Micas

These were a range of exclusive metallic paints that used silver and coloured aluminium flakes to provide a sparkly effect, with the size of the flake and its particular coating varying from colour to colour to give the desired effect. Each was a £1,000 option.

Today, there's a register of Monogram models and they're all extremely collectable, with the rarest colours attracting large sums of money at auction, especially those in Chromactive paint schemes – but the downside is the cost of repairs if they get damaged as the paint alone costs £500 per litre.

As a footnote, MG Rover design director Peter Stevens was a vociferous opponent of the Monogram paint finishes, which he said detracted from the cars' styling purity. In a 2018 interview with the author he said: 'To be honest I hated the Monogram "flip tone" paint finishes; most looked either grim or like fairground rides. The problem was that our Colour and Trim department was up at Longbridge under the Engineering offices whilst Design was down at Southam. Both Kevin Howe and Rob Oldaker would sneak into the C&T area and bully the poor designers into colour choices that we only became aware of when they were already applied to the cars!'

Original Monogram Colours and Descriptions (as per MG Rover's My2003 Colour and Trim Guide)
Monogram Chromactive

Spectre – a lighter alternative to Typhoon with lilac, blue and grey travel.
Typhoon – a dramatic blue with green/purple travel.

The 2004 ZT-T 260 British Motor Show car finished in Shot Silk, which replaced Spectre and had a more greenish hue.

Monogram Chromescent

Glacier – practically a pearlescent white with silver facets.
Mirage – pearlescent silver with gold layers and a cool pale blue aspect.
Gulf Stream – Magic Green, that flips from pearlescent olive to grey-blue.

Monogram Super Metallics

Celestial – a bright light blue.
Chatsworth – an elegant antique bronze-green.
Lagoon – a bold turquoise.
Nocturne – a greyed off-mid/dark blue.
Sunspot – a warm pearlescent yellow with deep ochre and light citrus effects.

Monogram Micatallics

Jubilee – a bronze gold.
Orange Grove – an intense orange.
Saffron – a shimmering coppery-gold.
Bacchus – a rich iridescent wine red.

A ZS 180 five-door in Monogram Saffron.

A ZR 160 in Monogram Biomorphic Green.

Biomorphic – a strong mid-green.
Chagall – a strong mid-blue.
Garnet – a rich glowing red.
Nightshade – a lustrous black with blue highlights.
Spice – a rich deep brown.

Monogram Super Pearlescents
Black Olive – a luxuriant dark green with movement to black.

Express Delivery – The MG Express

With the clock running down on attracting external investment, MG Rover Group turned to ever more unusual niches in order to prove it could still introduce new vehicles to the market even under extreme circumstances.

In 2003, alongside the quirky but innovative Rover Streetwise, it also unveiled two other new vehicles based on the ageing Rover 25 architecture, namely the Rover Commerce and MG Express.

The pairing was a last-gasp attempt to take the company into an all-new market, this time of the car-derived van.

Vans based on small hatchbacks were becoming a marketable prospect for small businesses, with the Fiat Punto Van, Vauxhall Corsavan, Ford Fiesta Van

Above and below: The MG Express was previewed with the High Speed Service Van (HSSV) concept.

Above and below: The MG Express was essentially a hot hatch with no back seats.

and Peugeot 106 XRDT Commercial all achieving moderate but worthwhile sales in the security, meter reading and courier industries among others, while the UK's flat-rate taxation system for light commercial vehicles also offered a tax incentive for those opting for a van instead of a company car.

The conversion was straightforward – it was based on the three-door Rover 25, but with the rear seat removed and a flat load floor integrated into the vehicle structure, with a mesh bulkhead between the driver and the load bay.

Right and below: The load bay of the Express was surprisingly practical.

The rear windows were removed and replaced by painted aluminium panels finished in body colour.

In order to launch the vans, MG Rover created the HSSV Concept, which stood for 'High Speed Service Van' and was essentially a ZR rally car with van body, used in support of the MG Sport and Racing rally team.

While the Rover Commerce was targeted at fleets and small businesses, the MG Express was aimed more at those who wanted to take advantage of a tax break, so it was offered with the full range of engines from the MG ZR and featured body styling in line with the rest of the ZR range, along with alloy wheels and half-leather sports seats. It was also keenly priced, with the entry-level Express 105 (with a 1.4 K-Series engine) costing £10,995. As a sports van, it filled a unique niche in the British market, but it was clearly a niche too far – in total, just over 800 Expresses were made, and only a handful survive, making it one of the rarest MG models still in existence – and the only MG van!

Facelift Models – MG's Final Fling

By 2004, the MG Rover range was looking extremely long in the tooth. The ZR and ZS were both four years old and were, in effect, facelifts of previous models launched in the mid-1990s, and while other manufacturers were racing ahead with technological developments, the MG and Rover models were bringing nothing new to the market.

To put things into perspective, the Rover 200 and 400 were introduced at a time when Ford was still selling Escorts, the Renault 19 was still in production, Peugeot had just launched the 306 and Fiat was launching the Brava and Bravo. By 2004, the Ford Focus was about to be replaced, the Renault Megane was on its second generation, Fiat had just launched the Stilo and the Peugeot 307 was getting a facelift. These were old cars, and there was no getting away from it.

By now, based on the BMW-era model plan, both would have been put out to pasture, but the proposed replacement models under BMW had not materialised. MG Rover had shown its vision of the future with the RDX60 – a proposed 45 replacement based on a truncated 75 chassis – but the development money wasn't there for an entirely new car and sales had taken a substantial tumble.

The problem was, developing a new car would cost money that MG Rover Group didn't have, and while the design and engineering expertise was there and a new car had gone as far as virtual, clay and show car modelling, to take the project further required investment from outside. The British government wasn't forthcoming, and MG Rover's senior management were working hard to attract money from afar. Indeed, in 2004, the company signed a memorandum of agreement with China Brilliance, a Shanghai-based automotive company that wanted a presence in Europe and was seriously considering investing in the British brand... for now.

Brilliance wanted to see that MG Rover was looking to the future, as indeed did other external investors that Phoenix Venture Holdings was talking to, so in order to keep investors warm and prove that MG Rover wasn't standing still,

The facelifted MG ZR.

The 2004 MG model range.

the company went ahead with a wholesale facelift of its model range, but delivered it on a ridiculously tight budget.

There was no money for major engineering developments and the TF sports car was still holding its own as the UK's best-seller in its sector so was left untouched, but the 25, 45 and 75, along with their MG equivalents, were given a nip and tuck to make them more up-to-date.

All three saloon models got a new front and rear end, which translated far better to the MG models than it did to the Rover equivalents.

The ZR got new headlamps and a revised grille, along with a smoothed-off rear end with the number plate moved from the tailgate to the rear bumper, while the ZT received similar treatment, the original twin headlamps replaced by single lamp units and a revised rear end that included some incongruous plastic trim on the boot lid. The ZS came in for the biggest chunk of modifications, largely because it was based on the oldest design, so again the number plate was moved to the back bumper and a smooth tailgate or boot lid added. The front end treatment was more involved, though, and included a new bumper and headlight arrangement that was far more harmonious than the other models.

There was also a new XPower body kit for the ZS, fitted as standard to the ZS 180, and while the Rover facelifts were considered no more attractive than the car they replaced, the ZS with XPower kit was a fine-looking car and carved

The 2004 MG ZS.

Above and below: The ZS with XPower styling.

The facelifted ZT, French spec.

The facelifted ZT-T.

an enthusiast niche of its own. A similar series of tuning parts for the ZR were shown on the ZR-X Concept car in November 2004, but the full set of body kit parts never saw the light of day as the company went under before they were finalised for production.

The ZT received very little in the way of interior changes – a new steering wheel and a rather domineering badge and a few subtle trim changes, but otherwise MG Rover's most up-to-date cabin was left alone.

The ZR and ZS, though, got bigger changes inside. For the ZR, there was a new centre console with the heated rear window and fog lamp switches moved to above the radio and a new instrument binnacle, with revised white dials. It was a subtle but smart update and cleverly used the old car's main dashboard moulding to keep costs down.

The ZS, on the other hand, had a more comprehensive revision as it was cheaper for MG Rover to introduce a completely new fascia than it was to keep buying in the original dashboard moulding, which remained Honda's intellectual property.

As such, it got a wholly new moulding incorporating new radio and climate control buttons, new dials, new switchgear, a new gear knob and white dials. It was the most comprehensive change, but it needed to be as the car on which it was based dated back to the early nineties. The climate control switches, as an aside, also went on to feature in the Pagani Zonda supercar – a rare claim to fame for MG Rover as it stumbled towards its rather difficult end.

Of all the Z cars, the 2004 facelift models are the rarest. They were on sale for less than a year before MG Rover Group's ignominious demise, and while their numbers are limited as a result, they're arguably less desirable than their

The ZR interior.

The ZS
interior,
German spec.

The ZT interior.

forebears (facelift XPower-kitted ZS excepted) as they're considered to be cheaply finished and a bit rough around the edges.

The facelift cars were a last-gasp attempt to attract external investment, and despite the ambition of the design team behind them, the desperation showed in the poor fit and finish. When MG Rover finally folded in April 2005, the last cars off the line were arguably the least lamented in 101 years of history – a tragic end for a company with years of British social and engineering history behind it.

The TF and SV – The Other Phoenix MGs

After it had launched the Z cars, the second phase in MG Rover's revival of the MG brand came with significant revisions to the MGF.

The new TF, which debuted in January 2002, used the same bodyshell as the F, but the most significant difference was that the original Hydragas suspension was replaced with a more conventional steel-sprung set-up.

This brought with it multiple advantages. First and foremost, it was far cheaper than the fluid-filled set-up, while it also allowed MG Rover to lower the overall profile, answering one of the main criticisms levelled at the F when it was new.

The MG TF.

Other changes included a revised cabin and a new front end, incorporating the family grille and a deeper rear bumper, though this had first appeared a short while earlier on the facelifted MGF.

There was also a new 160PS version using the same VVC engine as the ZR160, which was the most powerful F variant and went from 0–60 mph in less than eight seconds, along with the TF 120 which used the original F's 1.8 K-Series, and an entry-level TF 115 using a 1.6-litre unit.

But it wasn't the fastest MG sports car of the era, as MG's XPower Sports and Racing department was involved in a very different project. It may have seemed an unusual move for a company that was struggling to pay its bills, but in 2003 MG Rover bought the rights to the Qvale (formerly De Tomaso) Mangusta supercar, powered by a 4.6-litre Ford Mustang V8.

This would give the company two advantages: one – an entry into bespoke, high-profit margin cars and potentially the US market, along with the opportunity to compete in the production class at Le Mans; and two – a means by which MG and XPower's employees could prove their worth to the rest of the car industry, as engineers who could put their hand to pretty much anything, not just workaday saloon cars and their hot hatch derivatives.

The MG SV-R.

Enter, then, the MG XPower SV, closely followed by the XPower SV R, which added an extra 65 bhp to the original car's 320 bhp. The £60,000 asking price was quite inexpensive compared to similar cars, but it was also crude and unrefined. That's not to denigrate its appeal, however, as the SV and SV R were incredible machines in many respects – loud, exciting and rousing to drive, much in the raw and simple style of a TVR or Chevrolet Corvette.

Both were excellent halo models to help promote the volume Z cars, though the TF was also a decent performer in terms of volume. Even in the first quarter of 2005 in the run-up to MG Rover's ultimate collapse, the model was the UK's best-selling sports car ahead of the Mazda MX-5.

Z Cars in Motorsport – Win on Sunday, Sell on Monday

For a brand built upon motorsport heritage, it was deemed essential by MG Rover Group to return to racing and to do so as soon as possible after it regained independence from BMW.

It did so at quite a high level as well, thanks to Nick Stephenson's associations with Lola seeing the MG brand back at Le Mans back in 2002 with the MG-Lola EX-258.

With the Z cars, though, it was rallying and circuit racing that were seen as the key to promoting them properly.

The ZR rally car, previewed as X-257.

A Group N S2000 ZR, driven by Gwyndaf Evans.

The MG EX-259.

The ZS in XPower race livery.

In 2002, Team Atomic Kitten also ran two ZSs.

The rally car would be the ZR, with a 2002/3 works-backed rally team competing in the British Rally Championship in Group N, with Gwyndaf Evans, Tony Jardine and Natalie Barratt as its drivers. The ZR was competitive in its class and enjoyed a number of successes, and to this day still does. Of the twenty-one works cars made, over half are known to survive and are still used for club championship rallying.

The ZR also competed on the track in the BRDC National Saloon Car Championships, with MG Sports and Racing commissioned by 'Team Airconstruct' to build three factory track cars, though these were never a huge success. The ZR remains a popular track car to this day, though, with MG Car Club events in particular attracting a strong field of owner-built racers.

The ZS, meanwhile, became the face of MG in the high-profile British Touring Car Championship. Indeed, the development of the BTCC car was carried out as a top-secret project, with West Surrey Racing (WSR) building the 'MG EX-259' on MG Sports and Racing's behalf as the official works team operator. It entered its first race in June 2001, just days after the ZS road car went on sale.

Because it joined the series mid-season, the ZS wasn't eligible to score points in 2001, but it showed huge promise, with a victory on the Brands Hatch Indy Circuit in September being the only non-Vauxhall BTCC victory of that season. Initially, the works drivers were Anthony Reid and Warren Hughes, both experienced tin-top racers.

For 2002, four cars were entered: two for Reid and Hughes as works cars and a second team as 'Team Atomic Kitten', driven by Colin Turkington and Gareth

A later BTCC ZS in RAC-backed livery.

Howell. It was a good year, with MG second in both the teams and manufacturers titles.

The two teams continued in 2003, but dropped to third behind Honda. That would be the last year of works support due to MG's financial situation, but WSR continued to use the ZS in 2004, 2005 and 2006, even adapting the race car to wear the facelift front end.

There's a certain irony, then, in the fact that the RAC-backed WSR cars enjoyed their most successful year in the same year that MG Rover collapsed, with the orange BTCC racers taking the independent teams' title.

The WSR ZSs were sold off at the end of the 2006 season but continued in the BTCC with independent teams as late as 2008.

The End of MG Rover and the Phoenix Four – The Day the Music Died

The demise of MG Rover was a tragic event that, right up until its final days, looked like it was an unlikely last resort. After several aborted attempts to strike deals with other car manufacturers, Phoenix Venture Holdings (MG Rover Group's parent company) had signed a memorandum of understanding with a Chinese partner, China Brilliance Automotive, which was interested in developing the company's planned new models to not only gain presence in Europe, but to also give it access to models it could sell domestically, which included the existing Rover 75.

The Brilliance deal ultimately fell through, but there was still hope in the form of SAIC, the Shanghai Auto Industry Corporation, which had underbid

The China Brilliance deal fell apart, despite talks between both parties.

Brilliance but was after the same product exposure and engineering expertise. The Chinese car industry was on the cusp of breaking through into the mainstream, and skilled design, engineering and general automotive industry experience were valuable assets even against MG Rover's backdrop of falling sales and financial losses.

Having already enjoyed a number of joint ventures with General Motors and Volkswagen, SAIC was ready to buy MG Rover Group in its entirety, but subject to due diligence. Operationally, though, MG Rover was in dire straits, without enough money in the bank to pay its workers or get through more than another month's trading, so it was forced to the negotiating table with the British government in pursuit of a bridging loan to keep the company going until the SAIC deal could be concluded.

On 17 March 2005, Department of Trade and Industry (DTI) officials wrote to Rover and SAIC offering a loan and stipulating three conditions: that there was actually a deal, that the loan was repaid, and that the directors of Phoenix contributed. They received a reply from SAIC on 19 March stating its concerns: MG Rover's solvency, the redundancy and pension costs, and the need for financial facilities. At the end of March, officials from the DTI flew to Shanghai with a pledge of a £100 million bridging loan from the government. However, it emerged that the proposed government loan was only allowable under European Commission rules if it was repaid in six months. SAIC's worry over liabilities meant it wanted the loan to be extended for two years – until, it judged, the joint venture would be profitable.

On 6 April 2005, SAIC contacted the DTI to say that the position had become 'extremely bleak'. The following morning, Longbridge suspended production due to a shortage of components after suppliers stopped shipments to the company because of the uncertainty surrounding its future. Later that day, Peter Beale, vice chairman of PVH, urged the government to provide the loan immediately, while Phoenix's directors offered to provide £10 million of their own cash to convince the government of their commitment.

Later that evening, a surprise press conference was called at the DTI attended by Patricia Hewitt, the trade and industry secretary, and Tony Woodley, general secretary of the Transport and General Workers' Union (TGWU), where it was announced that MG Rover had called in the receivers. Initially, MG Rover denied that it had gone into administration and said that Ms Hewitt's statement had been premature, but by Friday lunchtime PriceWaterhouseCoopers were appointed as the administrators.

Mr Woodley said at the time: 'My members have had a pretty difficult time over the past five years but we always thought MG Rover would find a partner. Up to three days ago, I still believed that SAIC would be that partner. This is an absolute disaster.'

After talks with unions and the administrators, the government offered a £6.5 million loan to cover overheads and staff wages at MG Rover's Longbridge plant for a week. During this week the administrators had hoped to reopen negotiations with the Chinese.

The plant stood mothballed for months.

Rover workers begged the government to save the company.

But on 15 April, Ian Powell, one of the joint administrators, confirmed that they had received a letter from SAIC which communicated to the DTI that SAIC was not willing to acquire either the whole or part of the business on a 'going concern' basis.

He went on to say: 'In light of this important development we have concluded that there is no realistic prospect of obtaining sufficient further finance to retain the workforce while the position with other parties is explored. As we indicated earlier in the week significant redundancies will now be effected.'

That afternoon, the administrators confirmed 5,000 redundancies. Around 600 workers would be kept on at Longbridge to help finish some 1,000 cars before the factory was mothballed, while around 400 workers would be retained at the company's engine plant. The impact on the supply chain was also huge, with around 10,000 jobs at stake.

An MG Rover Task Force was set up, led by the chair of the Advantage West Midlands (AWM) regional development agency and by the end of April, a total support package of £150 million had been allocated by the DTI to cover redundancy payments, retraining and support for suppliers – a greater amount than the original bridging loan that may well have seen SAIC buy the company as a going concern and the source of much criticism directed at the British government.

Kevin Jones – The Man Who Turned the Lights Out

Kevin Jones was head of MG Rover's product press and PR at the time of the company's demise, having climbed his way up from working in the press garage at Austin-Rover. At the time of BMW's sale of Rover, he was heading up the Rover division's product and engineering communications. In April 2005, he was the last man to leave the building in the MG Rover Group sales and marketing department.

'When Land Rover was sold and we became MG Rover Group it was like two children being separated as orphans, I guess,' he said.

'Especially as those TUPE'd [Transfer of Undertakings – Protection of Employment] to Land Rover were quite smug about their presumed better future. For those [of us] TUPE'd to Rover, we were philosophical and resolved to getting down to saving this truly great brand.

'We moved very quickly [from Warwick] to the International House Bickenhill offices and surrounded ourselves with those of the team that were Rover and MG. The early days were unnerving, challenging and hopeful, but each day moved forward for the better. There were operational difficulties – with no bank support, for example, we had to keep our company cars for 18 months, but running an MGF was no hardship.

'From a PR and marketing point of view, while Longbridge was central to the new business, at the time we were happy at the offices near Birmingham Airport, where we'd worked previously, although we spent progressively more time at Longbridge while the sales and marketing offices were refurbished and

Kevin in happier times at the wheel of a Rover 200 for press photography.

Kevin went on to work for PSA under the Peugeot and DS brands.

landscaped for our arrival, before the move there a good six months or so later. When we got there it was great to have everyone in one place.'

When asked about the news that Alchemy had prepared its takeover bid, Kevin said: 'I was decorating not one but two bedrooms when the news came in at 9 p.m. that night, so for the next day at least I knew what to expect. It was a period of great uncertainty. One that was obviously much in the public's eye – despite being a private company, the interest in the company was always as if we were still public property.

'At the time, the Alchemy proposal looked unworkable and worrying, as it was to be a much different operation with a slimmed-down outfit. Inside [the company] it didn't court many hopes of success, though you can't be too selective when your job is at stake.'

So does Kevin believe, with the benefit of hindsight, that an Alchemy-style takeover could ultimately have worked for MG Rover Group?

'No, not for a second. While it would no doubt have taken some time to make the necessary adjustments, I think we all knew it was a façade for asset-stripping, as the ideas for the business took little of the niches and established business we already had in place, that MG Rover Group validated more perfectly.

'The irony was that this idea from Alchemy gave BMW the way out of the marriage. To ensure its future, when John Towers met BMW he warned of a likely eleventh-hour request for more money strategy, that questioned the integrity of the proposed offer, and BMW did wish to mitigate its decision with a fair and morally robust solution – irrespective of its need to protect its reputation in a key business market.'

But things changed as the Phoenix bid gathered momentum.

'Immediately there was a "can-do society" mindset,' said Kevin. 'It was made clear from the outset that we needed to maximise the return on investment and spend wisely with less, but that we had a good platform to build on, having launched new versions of 200/400 as 25/45 to supplement the still-new Rover 75. While there continued to be doubters, the majority [inside the company] were supportive of our aim to succeed, and it was a great national story.'

Had the new MINI been part of MG Rover's portfolio, Kevin believes things may have turned out differently.

'The goalposts were changed,' he said. 'When new MINI was originally with us to prepare to market, BMW ensured the price was lowest at £10,850, despite our protestations to increase it. Under their stewardship, they operated just as we had proposed, selling it for c. £12,500, but with the investment a new brand requires, with CAB2 also a factor, it was grand-theft auto, taking the best bits for themselves.'

Irrespective, Kevin said that the mood when the new Z cars did appear was suitably upbeat.

'With Rover established, it was natural to excite the company with a new range of MGs. These didn't take too long to evolve, and were all derived from the Rover models. In creating the 1.5-millionth MG in 2003 [a ZT] it was interesting

The new MINI was developed by Rover but ultimately became the property of BMW.

to realise that the saloons' popularity was two-thirds of the historic MG volume, and was surprisingly a fundamental aspect of the brand's core profitability.'

'The mood at the time was probably the first public moment that showed we were not broken, and capable of survival. Indeed, we had vigour and not one, but three "new" models. These were great days, including a press event held in Wales at the St David's Hotel, and with the MG ZT XPower V8 to show we had more to follow besides.'

So was Kevin, as the head of product communications, surprised at the positive media reaction towards the cars – the ZS in particular?

'The press, bless'em, know "almost everything"', he said. 'They knew a Rover 200vi and a Rover 75 were going to be a sound start for a performance derivative. What few believed was how good a tuned-version of the 45 was going to be. I took real pleasure seeing their faces of disbelief when they had driven [the ZS 180], helped by us demonstrating it on roads and then at the Pembrey Circuit to show it had "racing-potential".

'The press, once they'd driven them, were very impressed. They had branding, a high build standard, were affordable, powerful, much to like in fact. We also had a product growth plan, and a quick start – and with the prospect of motorsport to vindicate and promote the cars – very exciting, when you think of other brands with much less.'

The track performance of ZS 180 surprised a few journalists!

At the time of the Z cars launch, MG Rover Group had a very aggressive marketing plan, one that attracted some ironic parodies on the auto industry website sniffpetrol.com

'This brought ironic confusion,' said Kevin. 'The ASA banned MG for an ad about speed when any sign of speed was being frowned on, but the message was confused. Thus MG quickly appeared to be something of a 'rebel speed brand', and the enthusiastic drivers and Sniff Petrol website responded to it so well. It was all about attitude, and Sniff led the sentiment, helped by X80 and what became the MG XPower SV.'

Kevin also believes that motorsport was a core part of MG's image.

'Motorsport is a very good way to show that a product is competitive, fast and durable,' he said. 'With the speed of arrival of the MG Z cars it was always factored in to vindicate MG's pedigree. That said, as the Rover 200 was already active in some lower levels of rallying, it was natural that the MG ZR would follow and go further. With the ZS and the most underrated Z model, it was another, more prominent activity – with supplementary sponsorship opportunities in BTCC and with TV coverage it was a perfect brand visibility initiative.'

But optimism soon turned to reality for MG Rover Group's employees.

'Project Drive was a moment when we realised we were in serious times, as though savings are necessary, they do little to enhance the product and the saving on cost was not noticed by customers until too late. You can see the logic, but it's not what a brand ever wants to go through.'

Kevin takes a melancholy view on the final days of the company, which had been part of his life since he was a young man.

'While every day was one of those "how can we maintain this pressure and stress of work" days, in other ways we loved the speed, camaraderie and sense of achievement that just was not possible in bigger organisations. We all believed that we would find an investor and worked hard with SAIC to reach that point, but they were badly guided by DTI who had been burnt once before and were playing super safe. Never did we go to work thinking it was game over. Even when we got the extra week, we worked hard up to and beyond the last day.

'I decided I wanted to be there to the end, as like so many others it had been my life's work, so I stayed until 7 p.m. and turned the lights out in the sales and marketing offices... and then did the same again a week after.'

Footnote: Kevin Jones went on to become head of PR for Peugeot and DS Automobiles.

MG – The China Story

MG Rover died, but MG didn't. Instead, some of the cars went on to lead a new life in China, and MG returned to the UK market in 2011 under Chinese ownership, where the brand lives on as part of SAIC.

But it wasn't SAIC that bought the remains of MG Rover originally. Much of the engineering and manufacturing equipment along with the intellectual property was acquired by Nanjing Automotive, which went on to merge with SAIC in late 2007, meaning SAIC ended up with the remains of MG Rover after all.

Among them were the TF and 75, which was being sold in China as the MG 7 or Roewe 750, with the Roewe badge closely resembling that of the original Rover one. The company also developed a smaller car, the Roewe 550, off the 75 platform and this would also go on to become the MG6.

In 2009, SAIC dipped its toes in the water in the UK, opening an office in London from which it sold the TF 500 limited edition, essentially unchanged from the original. It also announced that, from 2011, it would bring manufacturing back to Longbridge in the form of a CKD (kit form) variant of the MG6, offered as both a hatch and saloon. The company had retained its engineering and technical centres at Longbridge and while it never resumed volume production, the ties to the 'home' of MG Rover were (and remain) inextricable.

Today, there is no core production at Longbridge, but MG's future looks more positive than ever before. The MG 6 has gone, but the MG 3 supermini enjoys decent sales and the new ZS – an SUV with nothing in common with the Rover

The MG6 was produced in kit form at Longbridge.

The MG3 has so far been a decent seller.

The current MG ZS bears little resemblance to the original.

45-based model – has seen impressive sales success. Two more SUVs and an electric powertrain have also been introduced. It's not the MG that was the original vision of the brand's forefathers, but it's fascinating all the same.

In 2017, 18 and 19, MG Motor UK was the fastest-growing car company in Britain in terms of sales volume and had increased its dealership network five-fold since its inception.

Classic in Waiting – Buying a Z Car Today
Whether it's the brand, the heritage or the fact that the MG Z cars were probably the last truly good cars to emerge from 100 years of Longbridge manufacturing, they have acquired a cult following as modern classics, especially with younger drivers. They're only set to become more collectable in the future, too. But buying one doesn't come without its caveats, especially as the cars get older. But what should you look for when buying one?

ZR
The baby of the bunch was the best-selling Z car and survives in greater numbers than the larger models, but it's not without its problems.

Rust has laid claim to many a ZR already.

With the exception of the turbo diesel, which sold in tiny numbers, all ZRs have the Rover Group K-Series engine, which has an unfortunate reputation for head gasket failure, a side effect of the engine's design having a far smaller coolant capacity than most of its peers, meaning any loss of coolant can lead to rapid overheating.

Many if not most of the survivors have had a revised head gasket fitted by now, so the problem isn't as rife as it once was.

Otherwise, the main things to look for are bad modifications (add-on body parts and 'tuning' components are common) and rust. The ZR suffers worse for this than the larger Z cars and can corrode badly around the back of the sills and rear wheelarches, as well as the front wings and floorpans.

ZS

As with the ZR, you need to be aware of potential head gasket issues, while the V6-engined ZS 180 requires its cam belts to be changed at 60,000-mile intervals. A snapped belt will kill the engine, but replacement is fairly complex and requires a few hours work at a specialist – something to bear in mind if viewing a used example.

Less than a quarter of the remaining ZSs survive, so rescue one now. (MG Car Club)

Rust wise, the outer bodywork is normally pretty hardy, but the ZS can suffer from corrosion to its front floorpans and bulkhead seams as well as at the back end of the sills.

ZT and ZT-T

The big Zeds were the better built when new, of that make no mistake, but in later years the mechanical and electrical simplicity of the smaller cars has made them the easier models to own.

Like the Rover 75 on which it's based, the ZT is prone to electrical niggles, especially if water can be allowed egress into the upper bulkhead where the ECU lives. If the drain channels get blocked with dirt and leaves, the ECU plenum fills up with water and a fried ECU is enough to write a car off completely.

Other electrical problems include instrument binnacles, electric window switches and dashboard trip computers, while trim components and bonnet releases can also be flaky.

Rust is less of a problem, though the ZT is prone to corrosion around the rear ends of both sills, so check this area carefully. It's a contoured panel, so repairs can be fairly involved.

Overall, though, the Z cars are generally pretty dependable and are less complex than many of their contemporary rivals, which has led to a surprisingly good survival rate. They represent terrific value, too.

ZTs really don't benefit from being left standing.